The Joy of Jazz

Jazz is American. It reaches every corner of the world. Performers interpret it differently. Yet it retains its unmistakable rhythmic, harmonic and melodic profile. It pictures the warmth of New Orleans. And, it relates the 'cool sound' with the tempo of the big city. THE JOY OF JAZZ depicts jazz development through the works of great personalities. For the first time simplified arrangements of Charlie Parker, Kid Ory, Thelonious Monk and Fats Waller are available to the student For the piano teacher and student this is not a frivolous excursion into the 'pop' field. It can be integrated with the regular teaching repertoire with excellent results. A few hints: Keep a steady beat throughout. Use little or no pedal. Play in the style.

Copyright © 1968 Yorktown Music Press, Inc.

US International Standard Book Number: 0.8256.8004.2
UK International Standard Book Number: 0.7119.0126.0

Exclusive Distributors:
Music Sales Corporation
225 Park Avenue South, New York, NY 10003 USA
Music Sales Limited
8/9 Frith Street, London W1V 5TZ England
Music Sales Pty. Limited
120 Rothschild Street, Rosebery, Sydney, NSW 2018, Australia

Printed in the United States of America by
Vicks Lithograph and Printing Corporation

D1412236

Love Somebody

Gerald Martin

4/12

Get Out Of Here

Kid Ory
Bud Scott

Lively "Dixieland" tempo

Won't Ya Come Out Tonight

Gerald Martin

Willy The Weeper

Denes Agay

9

Lady Bird

Arr. by
Frank Owens

Tad Dameron

Ev'ry Night

(Folk Blues)

Denes Agay

The Happy Organ

Ken Wood
David Clowney
James Kriegsmann

Maple Leaf Rag

Scott Joplin

Yes Indeed

Arr. by
Frank Owens

Sy Oliver

With a spirited beat

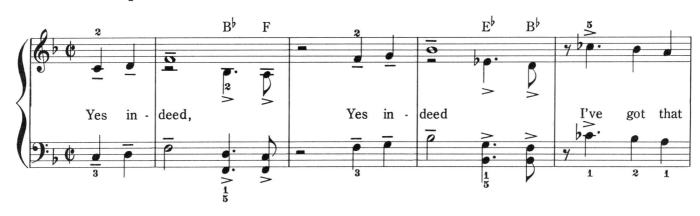

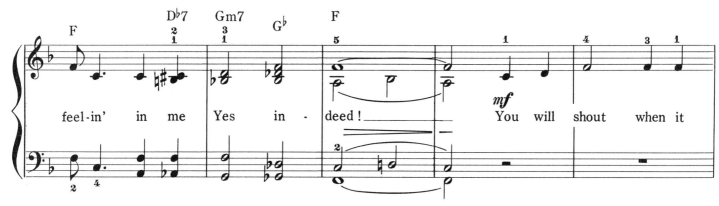

lu - jah,"   When it   hits you   you   hol-la "Yes in-deed!"

Stomping Down Broadway

Ernest Wilkins

Medium jump tempo

Blue Petals

Robert Dorough

Kicking The Blues

Ernest Wilkins

Opus One

Sy Oliver

Moderate jump tempo

Lop - Pow

"Babs" Brown

Moderately bright

Well Groomed

Charlie Shavers

J. D.'s Boogie Woogie

Jimmy Dorsey
Marvin Wright

Moderate boogie tempo

Easy Does it

Dave Martin

Sneakin' Home

Thomas "Fats" Waller

Things To Come

Dizzy Gillespie

38

Oop Bop Sh-bam

Dizzy Gillespie

52nd Street Theme

Fast

Thelonious Monk

Three Jazz Flavors

Moderate swing

"Salt Butter"

Erskine Butterfield

Slower with a lilt
"Sweet Butter"

Crisp and lively
"Peanut Butter"

Anthropology

Dizzy Gillespie
Charlie Parker

Palm Garden

Thomas "Fats" Waller

Slow blues tempo

Rollin' Rocks

Robert Dorough